In the House of Slaves

In the House of Slaves

Evelyn Lau

Coach House Press
Toronto

FIRST EDITION
Printed in Canada

Published with the assistance of the Canada Council, the Department of Canadian Heritage, the Ontario Arts Council, and the Ontario Ministry of Culture, Tourism and Recreation.

"The Songs of Adrian Zelinski" © 1988 Czeslaw Milosz Royalties, Inc. From *The Collected Poems* by Czeslaw Milosz, published by The Ecco Press. Reprinted by permission.

Some of the poems in this collection first appeared in the following magazines and anthologies: *Absinthe, Another Chicago Magazine, Canadian Forum, The Male Body* (University of Michigan Press), *Massachusetts Review, Michigan Quarterly Review, Newest Review, New Letters, Organica Quarterly, Poetry Canada Review, Southern Review, Verse, Witness.*

Canadian Cataloguing in Publication Data
Lau, Evelyn. 1971–
In the house of slaves

Poems.
ISBN 0-88910-468-9
1. Title
PS8573.A781515 1994   C811'.54   C94-930319-4
PR9199.3.L3815   1994

CONTENTS

PART ONE

"With what grace you always lend yourself to his follies! No other woman would do as much—no one! In this manner you will always keep him. One thing is funny, though: that it is you whom he calls 'mistress' and himself whom he calls 'slave'!"

—Wanda von Sacher-Masoch,
The Confessions of Wanda Von Sacher-Masoch

PRESSURE

If I rest my fingers here
if I lay my cheek like one petal
of a rubbery orchid against your cheek
will you rise from your knees
will you pull your wrists free of these leather cuffs
teach me the history of the stitches in your spine
that mole and the cold rims of your ears?
You are brown along your legs
red across the hills of your shoulders
only your buttocks stayed pale
under boxers you wore on a beach somewhere
on a handful of islands in the tropics
curling your toes in the sand
flexing the soles of your feet at the sun.
Your lips to my shoulder burn like a brand
in this room, where two stalks of orchids reach high like hands
and drop, and the sound of the air is soft
as the mushroom carpet
white as the lace you fling around your hips.
Here is the perfect stocking
here, clasp it
between the two buttons of the garter, rise on legs
cased in the shimmer of a butterfly's crushed wings
I can smell the powder in the air
I can feel you reach with the arms of dying orchids
your lips pursed like a cherub's
your face red with pressure
nipples clipped between miniature planks of wood.
Take it off, take it all off
wipe the tears that slide glass over your eyes.
If I strike a match will you pour flames from your eyes
birds of paradise red and orange at the sharpest points
will your mouth leak a kiss onto my tongue

to run down your neck and across your burnt shoulder?
At least touch my tongue
with your tongue, with some salt of remorse
at the corners of your eyes, cross your arms
behind my shoulder blades and press me close
so my stomach caves
at your stomach solid against me.
Hold my face in your hands, you burn
with the heat of vacations taken in winter
beaches advertised in travel agencies
grass skirts never the colour of grass but of autumn leaves
blue cocktails and a white sun to watch over you
year round, burning away symptoms of sadness.
Don't kneel, don't submit
with your kisses on these stockings I wear for you
lighter than breath
your hands shaping calves and the hurt of an arched foot
your eyes driving through mine, driving blue lightning
and I don't dare blink, I can't blink
I swallow the white shroud of this room
tug at the shroud of hair brushed back from your forehead
know you will leave with your nipples
matching the heat of your shoulders
the stripes of the crop cardinal across your buttocks
now simmering, then fading.
Don't say you came to learn about pain
when you will leave with all the colours inside me
wear them for days on your back and breast
like the branding of an island sun.

Nothing Is Happening

Kneeling with hands locked behind your back, you are not a forty-seven-year-old man ducking your forehead to the carpet. You are not crawling on your belly across the room to grip the handle of a drawer, to pull it open with your teeth, depositing a soft weight of slips and embroidered panties in my lap. It is not you pulling a teddy over your head, shimmying along the floor, your silk-covered buttocks moving as if under enemy fire crisscrossing above your body, the way this crop in my hand is not crisscrossing your body. In the mirror I do not notice my red lips like an open wound, my statue-white face or the elegance of my whip twirling in the air.

I am thinking about walking the cobbled streets towards Paddington Station in London on an April morning. I am thinking of the corner grocer in Europe who sold fleshy purple plums and a dozen newspapers, and who dispensed winks and directions for free. I am wondering if it will snow in New York in February and should I wear my new coat and bring a pair of boots. I am calculating what time it must be in other cities, what time it is here in this city outside this timeless hotel room with its view of a church, with its waterfalls and chandeliers and six elevators in the lobby downstairs.

I am not seeing you stand up, the silver bar unlocking clickclick and the leather circles wrenching from your wrists. Not sitting in a corduroy armchair tickling your bruises with the tip of a whip, not ordering you to masturbate staring at yourself in the mirror, a reflection of blue irises and a loose shoulder strap against your hairy arm. Inside these custard-coloured walls I am not screaming, Aren't you ashamed, a grown man wearing women's clothing, jacking off, buying a woman and making her watch you, making her hit you, making her— And you are not groaning, hard at the shame between your legs like you are hard at the shame burning a kernel in your chest, burning you alive. Profiled in lace and satin, your balding head beading with perspiration, you are not crying with urgency and I am not screaming now high above you, high as the ringing of church bells. Your body is not shaking, shuddering, your body is not blurring at the knees, not shivering inside satin, you are nowhere, you are not here in a manwoman crumple at my feet.

PULSE

Rain slants through the casement window,
black stains the brocade wall.
Behind the gag, your pink mouth gurgles.

I retrieve pins, razors from the debris at my feet
like I would stones or shells at the beach.
I clip a lock of hair, a nipple.

I hold a flame to the candelabra.
Open a bottle of resiny wine.
I bend to kiss the pulse at your wrist and throat.

In the House of Slaves

Slaves go flying through the house, through this house slaves crawl fast, hands and knees carpet-burned. Your house beside the university, red geraniums in the flower box and a squirrel who refuses the hazelnut in the palm of my hand. It is autumn outside the slaves' house, I leave nuts lined up like a trail of breadcrumbs outside the French doors.

In the bedroom the switch of the cat, the music of the riding crop under a painting of a woman in full skirts carrying boiling water to a naked English boy, buttocks turned to the painter, waiting for his painful baptism. Your eyes twin onyxes raised from where you kneel with hands glued in prayer, your eyes reflecting a darker season, some place far from here. Where it rains all the time. Dress shirt and tie pulled loose to disclose your body turning for inspection, front, back, into the kitchen with tiles ridged and bumpy under your palms, through the bathroom with its mosaic of naked women.

In the house of slaves candles striate the air above your genitals, falling wax like hot seed spilled across your loins. A squirrel hurries across the terrace to the safety of the maples, the spinning debris of autumn, other houses down the lane. On the walls angels leap with harpstrings slicing their fingers. Each morning I wake you with a round of slaps; each night you are chained to the bedpost, wrists and ankles shackled apart, leather conforming to your body. And through the house the bodies of my slaves lean as greyhounds, tubby as angels, running pure.

Your Garden Filled with Chairs and Stones

Your garden filled with chairs and stones, a place where friends gather in the summer. The backs of the chairs are like the backs of some women, indented with long gliding spines, empty-looking when not embraced. When alone.

Begin the countdown at 100 strokes.

I follow your man's ponytail, the colour of a chestnut, skin unpeeled, fruit falling solid into the furrow between your shoulder-blades. I follow your dirty neck into the bedroom.

Lie on the bed, like this, stomach down. Face turned away to simulate shame.

Your ankles wrapped in red and white fishnet, narrow feet with low arches folded one over the other like gloves. Your wrists motionless in the bracelets of new leather, so stiff I must apply lips and teeth to the straps, must pull and tug until my gums ache.

How many layers, epidermis, dermis, before finding you.

I lean into you but stand apart, my fingers splash metal and leather across your body. Straight black strands scatter across your skin, disperse in the four directions. Tips of the whip fling gold stars.

Your voice stutters when you reach the count of ten. And down.

Outside in the November chill, limousines pull in and out of your driveway with the languid air of cigarettes held and smoked in holders. In the courtyard the bricks are red but dry. If the curtains were open we would see your winter garden, a symphony of violin-backed chairs, conductors' signals of traffic flashed from the window frames, back out into the street.

If the curtains were open.

Yes, you say, the pain is difficult, and the centre of your voice is hollow as an empty jar.

In the light from the naked bulb, I lean over you to inspect my work, but only with eyes that could belong to anyone. I protect the rest of my face from the red glare lining the other side of your skin.

ON A BED THE COLOUR OF STONE

I wait for you on days that dawn mild and overcast, propitious days you call them. Days of rain that keep Japanese investors away from the golf courses so that you can leave work early, idling your gunmetal car outside the lobby. Under branches of cracked ice your face behind the wheel is cold and blue, hair drawn back by the teeth of a comb, eyes liquid in the bones and shadows of your face.

We walk into your house past a row of bonsai trees, into a living room matte grey as an eyeshadow. We drink liqueurs from the brass cart until the room is black, we enter your bedroom blooming with vases and flowers.

You on a bed the colour of stone, blue grey, mottled, myself in the mirror pale as rice paper against the northern brick wall. The smell of burning hair fighting the mist of flowers as I draw lit matches along the points of hair on your body and you lie still as ice over water. Biting into the pillow with the tips of ten fingers, your eyes bend like the surface of an ocean ruffled by wind, your body stretches across quilted stone. Tell me the princess story, you say, tell me again about being a beautiful princess in a faraway land, where I am a penniless wanderer locked in your dungeon, forced to breed a race of slaves for your amusement ... and I tell you the story while a skein of storm clouds races highspeed across your eyes like some dream sequence in a movie. I tell you I am a princess of silk and satin and full-figured laziness plotting tortures for you on slow Sunday afternoons. And when you escape I chase you on a thoroughbred through the forest, I find you quivering in some sunlit glade, I ride you home your hands and knees raw the perspiration of rage painting my face gold.

Under this aqua sky in this land where the sun turns the leaves of all the trees to emeralds, you are fed and fattened in your shiny cage. In Vancouver it rains all winter and already another princess is leaving her perfumes and lipsticks in your cabinet in the bathroom. Afterwards it is you who dresses proudly, in the ebony room smelling of orange brandy and freesias. It is you who turns the keys in all the locks when we leave, footsteps sounding under an enraged sky, past a dozen boxes of twisting stunted trees.

With your mouth you bring me weapons. The long-stemmed black rose of a riding crop. A taper candle. You crawl from the side of the bed, eyelids hung low in repentance. With your mouth you turn every doorknob until all I see is a line-up of doors, you kneeling to one side, ahead a haze of light. I walk through.

The coffee table a display of tissues and needles and a prim bottle of bleach. Bedtime stories, you call the sleeping pills, I have 50 bedtime stories for you tonight. Outside the windows a blossom of light, stamens of neon flaring against the sky; in every teaspoon a pool of blood and a pull of cotton.

The new leash wraps perfectly around my knuckles. One day I will leave you tied, wrists to posts, your eyes blue torches beseeching my face, the groans round and red as apples in your mouth. Meanwhile I dream of men thrown from balconies, men who turn into manuscripts bulky and sinking as if through heavy water, too late to catch without also falling twenty-five stories down to the ending. In the air your body the shape of a fiddlehead, unwinding. Your body slowly scrolling down, coming apart like old rope, coming apart in sentences long as limbs.

CHRISTMAS DAYS

Today is the last Friday of autumn, the radio said. You broke your body onto the bed arms legs spread-eagled, ropes with frayed ends pushed like camels through the rings on cuffs. Jeans and underwear off and the duvet slipped onto the floor. When you dared to laugh I slapped you, you said Ouch, the next time it was more a blow than a slap, and your head swung and your eyes went out like lights. Your eyes softened to the colour of plums. And your chin went down, your tongue went down along the toes of my boots, your kisses like butterflies perched on the black leather of my boots.

This was what you asked for, to be tied, to be tied face down, to be tied with a gag in your mouth. A ball in your mouth with straps running up your face over your curls down to the base of your neck and tight. So you looked like an angel in a painting, an angel perched on a pedestal peering over the cups of your palms, dimpled chins blondbrown curls the unrepentant baby fat of your arms. Your thick arms almost hiding the necessary wings.

You wanted to be no one to me, only the back of a head and a body, any body, a projection screen for hours of nightmares, rapes, slasher movies, years of loneliness. Your fingers gripped the brass railing, blossoming flowers of sweat. I touched the soles of your feet, they were wet with fear, my hand down your body came away shiny. I opened the balcony doors to chase out the smell of fear but it hung over the bed like a nuclear mushroom. A cold steamy sour smell rose from every pore. Outside it was December and a string of Christmas lights veered off someone's balcony and between the highrises of the west end the ocean closed its mouth.

The whip cut at your feet and you reached. And could not. The whip gashed your thigh and you curled your body thiswayandthat. It made a checkerboard of your buttocks, your skin went red where it was not white. I would not let you talk to me, turn your head, show yourself to be alive. The ball between your teeth a stopper for the words and sometimes the screams. It-hurts-me-more-than-it-hurts-you. And it did and I cried and my hands shook till the stroke of the whip steadied them. From behind the wall, from the next apartment, a brief knocking and then silence. From the city, west end seawall downtown, silence.

Later you were set free, ropes pulled, knots untied, cuffs unbuckled. There was blood on the sheets, so red, so festive. You ran your hands down your body with pride, touched a wounded nipple. I put my lips to the nipple, licked the seawater salt of your blood. And you sighed with your head thrown back, throat exposed and glowing, eyes dark and dazzled. At the door we exchanged Christmas presents, the red packages from you so many they spilled over my arms.

THE NINTH ORDER

The lids of your seraph's eyes lowered in the centre of the glass room. Light reflecting off the gold posts in a woman's earlobes scatters the shadows of angels across the ceiling. From behind a screen of leaves and branches it is not certain whether you have wings or even a face. I think your hair is yellow, that it fleeces your collarbone.

Your body in repose arcs like the bodies of male statues, knees tucked under, shoulders hilled. Your arms still, muscles and baby fat grained and grey as an old photograph. A pair of thumb cuffs slices two ragged halos into the base of your thumbs.

During punishment your mouth puckers like an angel's: No oh no oh please no. The welts form thin bars on which music notes hover, the looping grace of a treble clef and the ear of the bass. Around us women in white robes start to sing as you spin a garment out of your own blood, silk the colour of red wine, claret, port, flowing dolman sleeves down to your wrists.

Outside the glass room the snow on the mountains drifts in winged depressions, left behind like calling cards. Any moment now you expect to ascend to your highest order, and lift this dog collar up into a halo.

CRACK

Today you are wearing a white body marked vertically and horizontally with underwear, garter belt, stockings. You move unsteadily on the two black bars of your heels. A bald man sits on the side of the bed and plays with spoons and baking soda and cocaine. The mattress is covered in a single rough sheet the colour of camelhair. It is the only sheet he owns. He protects it with a beach towel when he thinks he is ready to come.

He turned the light on to bring you the dish of cocaine, and now you don't know how to turn it off. The room is swimming in a sickly yellow. The plate is made of a material that won't smash no matter how many times you throw it against the wall. Outside you hear cars passing and then something that sounds like thunder but it can't be thunder because through the blinds you can see a few mean streaks of light. You know it's sunny out there, whichever street this room faces. You know that out there is a familiar neighbourhood, full of faces you see every day lining up at the bank, posting letters, buying café au lait or a chef's salad from the bakery across the street.

The rolled bill is wrapped several times around with elastic. The powder snuffles up your nose, only a little more dense than the air you normally breathe. The aftertaste cuts thin bleeding lines down the back of your throat as it travels down. You massage your breasts with your hands and bend over the man on the bed. He removes his glasses and puts them on the bedside table where they won't be accidentally crushed. From different jars and saucers he spoons powder into a vial, then water; he shakes a flame under the glass and burns it black and brown across the bottom. Something is forming out of nothing, out of the cloudy water a nugget hardens and rattles with the sound of broken china between his rhythmically shaking fingers.

Somewhere in the neighbourhood there is a fire. Lights and bells burble through the streets; doors open and close in the rest of the building. He gets up to lock the bathroom and bedroom doors. He shakes the last drops out of a beer can, squashes one side flat and pokes ten holes into its dented side with a bent nail. He sprinkles cigarette ash over the holes and lays two cream-coloured cocaine rocks on top of the bed of ashes. He touches a long, flickering flame like a lecherous tongue to the rocks cuddled in their grey nest. You inhale through the opening at the top of the can, from which a gold bubbling beer should flow. You leave an impression of your upper lip in a ruby lipstick along its rim.

You stand up when he lies back on the bed and closes his eyes to the ceiling. You think you know that reflection in the mirrored closet doors—you are somebody you have met before, maybe you sat behind yourself in class a long time ago, or you are someone you saw on a television show that's since been cancelled. Through brown slits he watches you open your legs. Wider, he says. You gather one breast up in two hands and place your own nipple into your mouth. Good girl, he says.

ADULT ENTERTAINMENT

Hot in this apartment
even the paintings sweat
Moulin Rouge with its windmill
silver pillars at the end of a street in Oxford
a charcoal seagull and cloud cover over Paris
in every painting the streets are wider than they are in life
the passerby somewhere between shadow and substance
here the frill of a petticoat
there the skeleton of an umbrella

You live high enough
sometimes the breeze blows off the sea
across the Astroturf on the balcony
and knocks the blinds' plexiglass cord against the window.
I've seen these waterfront streets before
from some other man's balcony
the sulphur pyramids by the dock
the signs on the boxcars
time and temperature blinking from a concrete highrise.

Funny that you can tell me
to lie on your coffee table, paintings on either side of me
women flickering through rainswept streets
the blurred sway of shop signs above doorways
tree trunks bleak as cylinders rising from rock.
the oak table is the length of my body
sticky stocking-tops, slanting breasts
and disobedient nipples, this blur of a body
half-there like the sketched figures hurrying
through European streets on your walls
the edges of their gowns and jackets lifted by the wind
and the painter's brush

In this crisis moment I see all the small things
your mint-green shorts on the cedar floor
my silk shirt in a heap by the bookcase
our dismal reflection in the dark TV screen.
your hand clenches and unclenches
my legs are longer than shadows
the stockings lit with a light sheen
like mist on a windowpane.

I am ready to snap the birch switch
offer you an opened mouth
close my eyes against your oils and watercolours.
let me know when it's over, I will
rise and wash my hands with the jasmine soap in the bathroom
replace sunglasses and lipstick
hail a cab, hang my arm out the window
and laugh
the skies are blue, the money was good
we are lucky to live

CARS

You return from Toronto in a new car
with new controls, stereo blazing from buttons
pressed in the wheel, leather seats temperatured at your command.
Your house smells still of evergreens,
candy in glass bowls on the table,
wafers of dark chocolate, one white chocolate
like the flash of a thigh under a black skirt.
The Armani suit falls from your body,
folds onto a chair the way any suit might,
shapes of olive green and an exclamatory tie,
the sad dab of underwear on top, slipping
like a stunned bird to the floor.
Through the window I watch
a clench of crocuses open in a box,
purple crocuses growing in gravel outside your door.
Soon this daffodil will be out, you say,
flicking a white snarl of petal with your finger,
and these azaleas.

You arrive sleek in your leather driver's seat,
I walk out to meet you with leather around my hips
to register each print of your mouth and hands,
walk out not breathing into this freak winter
where blossoms drop and the street is bathed in blue.
Two ropes burn my palm and the flag of a whip
bumps my thigh. I walk on pebbles shining with sunlight
to your door, the smell of apples and dried peaches
in potpourri baskets, the smell of thick bathrobes
and Gucci cologne. My body fills yet I am drained
as a cup, as that wide land nicked by razors' edges
and lines of liquor left in glasses,
the desert landscape of a dream,
rock and swamp and a small child skipping.

I dreamt once of a man at the wheel of a blue van,
the background music of waves, traffic and water,
noise and night.
He washed his hair in a plastic sink,
slept two months of the year
with the Mexican sun on his belly, his toes tasting
of saltwater. The blue vans of my imagination
wait patiently in front of your window,
early cherry blossoms forming Japanese cranes
across windshields, under brutal tires.

The Narcosis of the Depths

Under the dark water, light. Clear streams intersect the ocean's bottom, pools tremble with the cool phosphorescence of fireflies. The narcosis of the depths: divers who push too far and begin to drown, reaching for a circle of lights and the faces that coax them down, fathers, mothers, lost wives.

On the waterproofed map on the floor you trace the crown of reefs where some day you may dive and not return. I touch Africa, the lady in the hat, and Italy, the boot, and the scatter of islands with names always unrelated to their shapes. The flecks and crumbs under my fingers are land masses in your mind; you research and penetrate their surrounding waters.

It is the best death, you say, because you think you are joining people you love who have come back to life.

I execute a shallow dive across your bedspread, try to focus drink-dizzy eyes on your face, backlit, as you push another corkscrew home. The look of a caught animal on your face when I cuff your wrists and ankles.

Soon I release you in a tangle, you overwhelm me with limbs and mouth and teeth that leave the famous red bruises. No pain, you say, no pain, not tonight. This time you want to leave for the islands unmarked, to undress in locker rooms without the other men looking. They all ask you, What happened. Last weekend someone guessed correctly.

If there was any other way, I whisper. My nails drive. In response your fingers deposit five prints along the back of my neck, under the fan of hair. The room tilts and drops.

Is this what it is like underwater? The walls black cliffs rising and your face the face of an angry aroused fish, the line of your nose higher, the mouth open in a shout that never breaks the surface of sound and rescuing light. Your hair floats a torn skirt over your forehead, I take your hand and guide it around my neck, not gentle, blue waves rise and batter my limbs, I brush coral, horns of coral spear the fetishist's dream of a wetsuit, through clothing to skin.

Hurt me, I say. The room washes somewhere between darkness and light, on the verge of breaking through. I want to break through, live on the side of light, the gathering voices, father, mother, home. As your fingers wring out oxygen I think I hear the voices calling, the walls bang together as if in a storm and the dark closes in.

Eyes hallucinatory, lips yawning into a smile, you swim through layer after layer of water towards the woman waiting between the cutting coral. Your fingers squeeze my throat till water rushes into my ears and through and I start to hear the clamour of the lights, loud, your fingers closing hard around the woman so she can't escape, not this time, no. Your skin breaks and I choke out a mile-long string of white soundless bubbles, and swallow sea water like wine.

Where Did You Learn

In your room overlooking the beach
I stand ringed in black lace bands
the blinds clap above the radiator
salt air and visions of sailboats blow through the window
your hands tear at my hair at my breasts
at so many frustrating buttons
outside the meticulous blinds, the sound of tires on a wet street
swipe of windshield wipers
two or three people walking on the sand

Where did you learn this hate
where did you learn
the sinister suggestion of a belt loosened
the clink of the cold buckle
outside the rains are returning like streetsweepers
the popcorn stands are being closed up
and wheeled away, the water is a grey
plastic sheet broken by concrete islands

Afterwards I want only to be clean
to pump pearly soap out of the container in the bathroom
to tease out underwear from the pile of clothing by the toilet
I want to emerge innocent in a towel and turbaned hair
to walk onto a white iron balcony somewhere
with blue skies, ocean air, orange juice
maybe even a man, waiting against the railing

NYMPHOMANIA

When I return from the island, the world
of the apartment complex is the same,
fire alarms and piano music in the hallways,
the successfully stunted trees in the Japanese garden,
even the mountains which have been admired to death.
Here is your withered body in the mirror,
my fingernails bright as sores on your skin,
the stiff strings of your hair tensed with gel and comb.
But do you never wash between your legs any more?
And where do I put my tongue
so the tastebuds that register sour and salt
avoid contact with the erection that looms
or flutters gaily in the ashen light from the hallway?
Too much for me. And never enough.

Red sand, red silt in the water,
the stages of the beach: grains dry and packed,
squeeze of chocolate mud between toes,
purple sea. Watch out for the jealous insect
following us from footprint to footprint,
watch for anything that bites or slashes.
I spend the afternoon killing snails,
eliminating their oozes, trickles, smells.
Some mornings in hotel bathrooms I torture small animals.
It's a small issue, nothing
to go into therapy about.
Only afterwards I feel white as the tiles,
silver as the taps, and somehow thinner
when I open and shut the door behind me
and go into the indifferent hallway.

Searching for something not yet named, how often
will I return to your bed and a hundred others?
By now the cab drivers know my wardrobe well.
I tell them about the island, though escape
isn't easy to explain, its bright ticket
thrust inside things like a blade, not easy
when every one thing means another
and still another beneath that other thing.
We can only be silent. This is better,
you settling down on the blue couch for the midnight movie,
my hands in my own lap,
yellow cabs in the monochrome street.

Part Two

Somewhere there are happy cities.
Somewhere there are, but not for certain.

—Czeslaw Milosz,
"The Songs of Adrian Zelinski"

A VISITOR

In the afternoon I kissed your wife, handed her flowers —
forests of limegreen stems, branches starred with leaves,
blossoms that trailed wisps and tendrils
down the hallway to form pools over vases, jam jars.

Grey had grown in her hair like moss bred in a moss garden,
mixed with yeast from yogurt or beer. You caught this hair
in a clump in your hand but it was not emerald or bright.
Still you smiled love at her, this ballerina with the aged hair,

all her bones gesturing inside the costume of silk.
You crooked your arm around her, tugged her close and down.
You were wearing a shirt I had seen on several men this season,
linen, the colours of rose and stone, of petals and ash.

Six steps up the staircase I waited for you to follow,
to open your mouth on mine, wetting my chin and nose,
your pale mouth somehow lacking the fineness of your mind
and the heart drumming in your chest.

I, a girl buttoned in black, supported on chunky heels,
with a face like a purse: the eyes open clasps,
the cheeks willing to yield to the stuffing of a tongue
and more. You looked at me as if to hold me down.

Instead you moved to the column of the fridge,
busied your fingers with the spiral staircasing of a corkscrew,
stems of glasses blowing bubbles between your fingers.
When your wife laughed and threw her fingers into the air,

I saw she was thin as the membrane on the wings
of some flying things, and I thought at any moment
her silks would balloon. Then she would drift high and hang
with her spine along the ceiling, and see down, see things.

THREE

Whole days of sunshine, like whole oranges.
You spend your holidays in beachside towns,
towns named after saints, populated by people you know
but choose to ignore. After waking,
your wife walks bare-legged to the doorway,
a white bathrobe cinched at her waist,
steam pouring up to her face from the mug of coffee in her hand.
There is a cedar table in the room, maybe a bowl of porridge,
definitely flowers from an exotic climate.
The sun is just about to rise, to pour its honey
over everything, the town, her skin.
And you the husband, coming up from behind,
hands caressing her shoulders so the bathrobe
nudges open in a triangle down her chest.
Not that we see this, we see only the tension in her neck
as she arches back in anticipated pleasure,
and the extraordinary abundance of your hair
as you bend to kiss her. As much pornography
as paradise allows behind its stage-set gates.

Stale airplane air, leg room in the first-class cabin.
The polite brightening of your eyes
as a stewardess stops to adjust something nearby,
a pillow or a fallen pair of eyeglasses.
From beyond the window, spatial morning light
squares across your face, across the front of your shirt
where a lipstick stain still lingers.
You might catch it in time, you often do.
Ahead, the impatient city waits, its fleets of taxis
running rivers of motion and stall in the streets.
You stow your baggage, reset your watch,
reach for the biography you bought in the airport bookstore,

breaking its spine so its cover bends back
over a thousand pages of memory.
The usual story. Ambition and regret,
family and outside success, a vow to remain faithful
to one face glimpsed for an instant in the plenitude
of faces in the changeable streets.
You shut your eyes: the murmur of a passenger's headset,
whiff of Obsession and the in-flight meal.
In transit, between women, you abandon yourself to sleep.

Sunlight through a hotel-room window in my own unknown city.
Taxis flowering in the dawn streets, clouds flurrying
across the buffed windows of banks in the downtown core.
This moment is reproduced with difficulty:
a woman's shape at the dawn window,
the hotel curtains thick and satin between her fingers,
the streets below her foreign as Europe
in this unaccustomed light. How do we show her embarrassment,
her awkwardness in her own body,
as you watch her from the unmade bed?
How do we show your natural inclination towards cruelty?
There is the full-length mirror on the wardrobe,
your hands on either side of her face
as full morning light floods the floor behind you
and you tug at her hair as if drawing her back
through the tunnel of increasing light.
We must show her discreet stepping away,
her feigned surprise at the hour on the bedside clock.
Gathering clothes, steadying herself for your departure,
bright motes of dust and air
like tossed confetti float and settle round her.

SMALL HOURS

Sometime I must have seen the sun go down,
sometime inside this night
of sedated eyelids, the remaining sighted world
condensed enough to tolerate
behind smoky windows in long blue limos,
in the back seats of cabs
behind the stringy hairs on the head of the driver.

Sometime the sun turned and toppled
through a blood-soaked bank of cloud
above a bay as blankly beautiful as the face
of some woman not involved in something
being done to her in bed.
The sun rolled off the tip of the sky,
piercing the gargoyled apex of the bridge

as I rode towards a concrete balcony
where you appear at two a.m.
when there is no longer any sun or stars
left in the sky, only shadows where trees grow black
at night, only drained streets,
the abandoned neighbourhood church.

Then your ankles cross on the circle of green glass
on the coffee table, and your fingers loosen
around the forgotten glass in your hand,
the sudden knock of the sleeping pill
meshing wall and ceiling. Some time ago
the dropped sun had sunk, deflated,
and now clouds fly across the sky,
while behind my lids I watch a theatre,
all the translucent red nonsense that precedes sleep.

PERSPECTIVES

In that last year of elementary school
I learned the art of painting in perspective.
This was after the self-portrait in pencil and charcoal,
the small-scale city home and country cabin,
the father's cast-off work shirt twisted into blossoms,
mandalas and rays of sunshine in vats of dye.

Tonight, I drive away from the perceived large thing:
the man left standing in the hotel-room hallway,
tugging his hair tight away from his face,
pacing, hands shaking, unbuttoning his shirt.
I pass billboards advertising detergent effective in cold water,
I pass a church sign announcing an upcoming ceremony of ashes.

Years before, I had drawn for our class assignment
a neighbourhood viewed down a narrowing strip of street,
automobiles dwindling down the avenue
until they could have fitted one over the other
like Russian dolls halved and boxed body over body.

There came a point in my picture where things didn't end
but became invisible to the ordinary eye.
I represented that point with a dot, as if it was an ending,
though all activity continued into the distance,
though all continued formed and standing,
long after it stopped being anything I could touch or see.

Like the man standing in the hotel-room hallway,
leaning his forehead against wallpaper,
taking a drink from the minibar,
moving resolute and alone
to his own unknowable bed at the room's centre.

Transition Phase

For a while his calls came, welcome as coins tossed
into an open case in front of a street musician,
silencing the downtown street
until the coin-giver moves on and melds
with the rest of the city's faces that you pass each day
and never find reason to congratulate or offer solace
for their daily triumphs or trials or their larger sorrows.
They who are like passengers on a bus that passes you
in the blue evening, profiled in yellow light.
So many pass you in this fashion
that you grow secure knowing many more will—
one street full of anonymous faces and light overcoats
will be replaced by another tomorrow.
Why then the tug at the lower portion of your heart,
the deposit of loss inside that cavity?
Is it the still phone, the distance of his city
preparing itself with boots and scarves for winter?

For some day these things will fade to amusing
vignettes of a less than halcyon time —
the phone calls behind closed doors,
drinks in lounges behind tinted glasses,
meetings coordinated in other cities with minibars
and a few available hours before dawn and the first boardroom.
From obsession a respite will eventually be reached.
No longer will you walk the grid of sidewalks
during lunch hour and feel his precise if invisible
presence beside you, past the white garbage pails
of flowers in front of the neighbourhood grocers,
past the butcher's shop and the designer clothing outlet.
You will come to think of him only in the lapse
between nightfall and the first dream,
between sleep and first light in the window.

TEMPTATION

The spare lines of your body
unfold along the couch, compress
into a single line on the floor,
cigarette smoke circling like silent mosquitoes
before a storm,
the break of rain over monstrous trees.
Here are so few words
to pinch and press between pages,
so few words but the blue drawings on the table,
your face stretched into the shape of a leer
or the flat deep surface of concern,
your mouth closing in and veering at the last second
from a collision, silver hair shaking over your eyes
and shining between my fingers,
like an angel's,
like tin foil. I am silenced by the uncounted kisses,
this thing that is not wonderment, temptation perhaps,
green cologne, smell of woodsmoke.
Yet how ridiculous it would be to see
the ribbon of your smile uncurling
in a morning ripe with butts in an ashtray,
strata of smoke near the ceiling,
the angry noises of daylight.

THE MONKS' SONG

Once my father heard the monks sing
in a Buddhist temple. At home afterwards
he paced the living room up and down
singing their song
while my sister's bare legs hung over his shoulders
and his hands held her
behind her small tight knees, held her in place.
He was wearing pyjamas that floated through the room
elegantly as any fashionable suit
though they were torn at the thigh, and a flap of cotton hung down
like the skin of a wounded animal.
The monks had misshapen skulls
beneath their shorn hair, they walked round and round
in robes the colour of dark wine
and sunshine in the middle of the day.
Some worshippers carried incense, perfume streaming
from the tips of lighted sticks,
up the stone steps, past the stone lions, inside.
My father took no pictures
though the day was bright as the flash on a camera.
His face was flushed with the autumn heat
as notes from a flute stretched like string
along the corridors, around the circling monks.
I remember their song, he hummed it for days afterwards,
it was one of the last times
his eyes were shiny as bells, ringing
from some region around his heart.

Towards Morning

At this hour the windows
across the street reflect nothing
not the pink grapefruit flush of dawn
not the sequence of clouds like a highspeed
chase from one executive's office to another
not the lengthy mournful veil of rain.
It is only night
and the streets are tired
the back of the chair a satin stripe
against your neck, your hair the smell of clouds
wide-bellied with rain, the smell of suits
balanced on embossed hangers, the sunsweat smell.

Now you try to sleep
discreet at dawn with the locked door
the curtain sheer as a woman's skirt
blowing around her legs down to her sandalled feet
blowing her around the seawall while the ocean
turns green like a vast disturbed eye
changing colour in sadness or contemplation.
At dawn the water is plucked free of sailboats
the mountains are icy as wishful dreams
dreamt in the middle of July.

As the sun goes about
lighting the corners of the sky
lighting your face on the pillow
flowers run wild by the sidewalk outside our hotel
matchstick flares of thistles and thorns
the nude thrust of stamen
the drop at the tip, the diamond.

COLD SHOWER

Showering in the dark, your body pivots
behind the transparent window of curtain,
a slip of soap in your hand, the smell of Ivory
a heavy white flower hanging in the air,
in the motes of dark filling up this porcelain bathroom,
floating feathers to the ceiling.

I met you in the bushes outside your home,
stepping on slabs of stone cut into diamonds,
rectangles wavering as if under water.
A snowdrift of children's coats cluttered the hall,
one diminutive denim jacket hung in a closet
like the jacket of an organ grinder's monkey.
The giggles and the whinings
of four absent daughters filled the house,
threads of music spidering the vaulted ceiling,
spinning down to your bent head,
weaving blond hairs around my body.

The bathroom is a vault filling with night
gleaming on curtain and washstand.
The head of the shower bursts its seeds of water,
your tubby body turns
and groans and squeaks in the shower,
blurs of bubbles dashing from you.
You rub your naked head downy under a towel
while I wait and play with your wife's makeup,
learn she glosses her mouth with rose petals,
leaves bare the skin around her eyes.

My Tragic Opera

Your home is the house with the leaded windows
gleaming gothic as flames toss in the fireplace.
Your bed is white as the whites of your eyes,
white as egg-whites, in the tomato-walled room
of the kitchen where you stand,
the neck of a bottle of Chivas in your hand.
The eerie blue light of your eyes wavers in the dark
as I make my way towards you holding my ice-laden glass.

Across the street, a line of empty houses on the block,
hooded in the snow that hides flaws in the foundations
and the painted structures. Yet sales remain slow.
Your real estate signs stay stabbed in the ground
like stakes or crosses, as you take me out
onto your newly-built porch, as my thinly-clad feet
sink deep into the punishment of snow.

But to fuck you in your nuptial bed while your wife
and children toss in hammocks in the tropics!
Upstairs, evidence of your daughters everywhere
in Doc Martens, denim and Beverly Hills 90210 pinups.
The eldest has starved herself beyond menstruation,
the middle one is the compulsive liar,
only the youngest remains a virgin in her white party dress.

Watercolours framed from first efforts in kindergarten,
drugstore alarm clocks, rows of pencils with erasers
that smell of peaches or passionfruit —
Don't tell me these things don't belong to me!
I will become bulimic and purge into your daughter's toilet,
sing my tragic opera in the shower with the reflective tiles,
lower my wifely bountiful body into the bath ...

Along the Oregon coast an 18-year-old prostitute
lurches out of a bar, aims her thumb in the direction
she wants the road to take her, is raped then stabbed
as many times as the years she was old. In extreme cold,
a plastic object will shatter at a single touch.
Tonight the city is crippled by ice, cars mumble
through the side streets, their movements precarious
as those perfect high notes in the opera at the coliseum.
Laughing, I test all your daughters' beds for comfort,
steal their lunch money, destroy their teenage trinkets.

Obsessed

Even in a dream grey as the ozone day
she calls you forth to touch your shoulder,
hoping that you will not turn away, resist her.
You do. For this she follows you
through the blacklit lime strata of club nights,
streets fogged with oyster-coloured lamplight.
Days papered with faxes, memos. She says no
to most men because they are not like you,
tells them there's nothing the matter,
nothing anyone can do. Often she remembers
your arms clasped around her knees in an open doorway,
forgets the band around your wedded finger
smooth and circular as fate. When it is late
she imagines you there in the spent day,
pouring the wine, peeling the anxious faces away.
She sleeps again, to make you appear,
kneeling at the end of a long swallowing hallway
of bevelled mirrors, florists' bouquets.
You are unclasping your hands, holding them towards her,
turning her around, all the way
around—changing everything—the gold loop broken,
fate denied, everything immutable gestured aside.

WINDOWS

Once, in a year of recession, we sat in a lounge
by the ocean, the marine air glazing the glass
and then your cheek. Both shone like silver whistles.
I was delirious, in love with the shadow your suit cast
on the sandy path outside the hotel, the way
the glass tilted in your fingers under their exact caress,
slight pressure that seemed to press
behind the hinges of my knees, where I sat in my seat.
You looked across the water to where last light bloomed
between two islands, brilliant as a bridge.
Out on the dock the lanterns swung at night,
and the faces of men and women, lost in their affairs,
drifted white, watery across the black window.

Universal Studios Tour

At the outset, a man in a gorilla suit
shambles down the length of the tram, trailed by a boy
with a camera affixed to his hand. For a price
I can see my startled face flex at the click
and flash of his camera. Then we are off.
The tram never diverges from its programmed path,
only pauses as though for breath at each site.
The teenage tour-guide lifts her lower lip
to blow at her bangs, scattering them like wheat
across her brow. I think of the years in school,
girls stalking between the aisles of desks, peering from
beneath their bangs. Outside the classroom, sounds
of games in progress, bells ringing recess.
Here, we stop to shudder at corpses in the lake
below the trick bridge, sharks with brutal faces,
admire the false fronts of saloons and mansions
on false streets, slyly curved at either end
to hint at further streets, instead of dead ends.
Through various worlds we rock, tilt, pause and pass,
until we arrive at the working studios,
their janitorial colours like the colours
of high-school hallways, olive and spoiled cream.
As we rumble past, the tour guide holding a finger
to her pouting mouth, we pass close to people
who still walk and work here, who sometimes look over
at us and wonder what worlds we come from
as we pass through the one they occupy.

False Creek

The mountains in the middle of the afternoon
frame your home in False Creek,
model cars in glass cases,
marble floors streaked pink,
a pendulum standing in a grandfather clock

Night falls suddenly,
covering the face of the ceramic frog
in its nest of bonsai and rock,
on the patio of a Japanese restaurant
where you burn your fingers on a bottle of sake.

You mount your bed,
eyes no longer squinted against the sun and scotch fumes,
irises grey as polished concrete,
as the floor of a restaurant with dripping candlesticks
and clocks with numberless faces.

Outside the French doors,
night reclines on chairs bleached to bone,
geraniums overflow their white pots.
You sleep beneath a sprinkler on the ceiling,
your heart and sex swathed in a Tokyo hotel robe.

WEST COAST

You'd like this chair, these walls, the rain sliding down
through the black evening. There are gimmicks
in the good restaurants that make the evenings worthwhile:
a pink stone to support the bamboo chopsticks,
a plastic folder to zipper up the bill and change.
Remember the night you said I had a change coming?
I heard you so clearly your voice was like a bell
tapped inside a cave, just as the lights
dimmed along the black lacquer bar,
and rain wet the windshields of cars parked outside.

Now, nights are clear where you are,
and a few miles east it has begun to snow.
Convertibles left topless overnight
amuse passersby and newspaper photographers.
You stay optimistic, you choose a seat by the window,
order a drink that sparkles, though this restaurant too
will disappear in the recession before the end of the year.
It's milder out here. The lounges close later,
drinks are collected, the last hour is called
when it is already day, eastern time.

You Said Love

I was eating chocolate sorbet at the Odeon
when you woke and said love.
It left me sprawled like Christina in her world
with the black farmhouse in the distance,
the hay in her hair and nose,
left me in my seat in the Astor Place Theatre
while toilet paper fell from the ceiling under black light
and I saw a face between the lightning strips of paper.
It wasn't your face I was seeing.
The drumrolls grew, paint flew
from the red and yellow drums on the stage.
Blue men climbed ropes and climbed ladders
while tubes twirled and Christina was sucked into a vacuum,
the field left empty but for the house on the horizon.
You said love
while I tossed back tequilas like golden grapes.
Swinging on a barstool at Costello's, tracing the Thurber walls
with my thumb, touching a linen sleeve but it was not
your sleeve, I pulled up a cherry by its stem
from a Tequila Sunrise and someone said
It is no longer sunrise it's too late and I said
It's too late

Four months of blackouts later you were saying love
with blue eyes, on your knees your hands huge
on my knees and I was on the Empire State Building
with only a ten-mile view that day,
sneaking through unauthorized passages,
climbing ladders and ducking under wire mesh,
some man beside me, not you,
some man spreading his arm over the city,
There is Macy's, there is Brooklyn, there is New Jersey, there—
You were falling, your arms around me in the blue van,

I was trying to leave without pulling your strings,
pulling your tendons your veins your nerves with me
to the lit lobby, holding your bloody strings in my hands.
I was one hundred stories higher than you
with only the crisscross of a grate between myself and you.

On Brooklyn Bridge I sat down
and looked to Wall Street and looked to the green figure
in the distance holding the spark in her hand.
You said love and I walked the bike path home with men flying
on bikes on either side of me, and everyone walked home
holding scarves over their faces,
pouring across this bridge stretched out like a song.
When I looked back the wind tore at my cheek
and steam trickled and poured out of all the gutters
and vents in Brooklyn, steam the smell of hot-dog water
in my eyes and nose. I walked inside the steam
into a waiting cab. When you said love
I was away, and dreaming, the sun flashing
on my snowy pillow where I was, where you were
the sea air dark on your dark beard.

PORN

Noon in California, bristling with heat and palm trees.
Dusty billboards, posters behind plastic, silver varnish
on fire hydrant, bicycle rack and marquee.
The ticket-seller in his booth counts change with one hand,
consumes sweets with the other, artificial colour
coating his fingers. Hotel in Hollywood, view of cheerleaders
practising their routines on the high school field,
bungalows and walk-up apartments, a police helicopter
circling above. The girls filmed in this historic suite
smoked cigarettes, wore garter belts, fishnets.
Where are they now? The one with the longest pair of legs,
the one with the broken tooth,
 the one who wore blue eyeshadow and moaned the loudest?

CITY AT SUNSET

A late courier appears at the office door,
the brightness of the horizon diffusing behind his blue uniform.
Like a halo, you think,
and sign your name next to his forefinger —

    A bookseller stands stunned in the street,
    mannequins twitch in department-store windows.
    The leaves on the trees are knotted
    with veins, aflame with the season.

A carnation slips crushed from the fist
of the street-corner preacher, his black book aloft,
the sun a gift of gold coins in the air
and his starved arm pushing a book skyward.

    Vision of pornographers' streets,
    condoms and X-rated dominatrix magazines.
    The stereo owner rubs his eye behind the dust-grimed counter,
    sips espresso, yawns. But it's you who I want —

you with the tie waving at some other person behind your shoulder,
you who are heavy with shopping bags and sated,
you who keep secrets behind your upturned collar —
a passenger on the path of disappearing light.

BLUEBERRIES

They gather in coarse cardboard baskets,
escape between your fingers and down your palms.
These dull sullen blueberries
already feel the chill, the frost fur
of the freezer on their skins —
lidded with apprehension, they huddle together
on separate stems.

The man weighs your purchase
in the shed with light muted through the window,
stench of newspapers, tang of raw wood.
You watch the scales tip and nod,
another dark purpling handful
and another, until the click of the scales,
the shiver of a spider on its thread.

You drive the highway home
with a twenty-five-pound box in the back seat,
a trickle of sweat stinging your eye
like a stray strand of hair.
Beside the lake which, today, shines and smells of salt,
fingers of light pluck at the fruitless bushes.

FAMOUS

Heat-haze nights, purple sky, palm fronds
crackling on the boulevards like lightning. Up in the hotel
girls' legs dangle out the tenth-floor windows,
opera bursts from the alarm clock on the nightstand,
cigarettes are extinguished beneath posters of stars
with glossy hair, cheekbones incisive as your own.

Outside at night on the path of pink stars,
Mexican men go cruising in their dirty white cars,
men with coiled bodies ready to spring to attack
or into a fit of dancing. The late-night liquor store
sells American candy bars in big print wrappers,
pocket knives and lottery tickets from under the counter.

Here you give speeches, attend receptions,
mingle with women in the lobby whose dresses spangle
at the shoulders and thighs, men with bossy shoulders.
Between two pillars, across the patio,
the famously reclusive actress sits and smokes,
legs crossed, jacket falling open to expose her breasts.

INDIAN SUMMER, 1992

Everyone talked about you those days
by restaurant bathrooms or on the curved stairwell,
over plates of chorizo on Italian patios. In the evenings
there were dinner parties to attend,
autumnal displays of catered food,
eucalyptus in olive oil cans,
corn cobs checkered with black and white teeth.
How quickly familiar, the sound of doors
opening and shutting in the lofty street,
the favouring smile of the prettiest woman present,
the social drunk's alarming gestures.
Though asked, you never did come
to wake us from this busy slumber,
the air kisses before and after,
the promises of contact, sometime soon.

SOLIPSISM

I spend days at the gym enclosed by four mirrors,
a silver pole balanced on my shoulders.
I slide keys out of the machines, slot them lower
to lift my weights with increased strain,
to pump the last reps in my personal program.

I watch on television a show that is being taped
in the studio across the hall. It is shown simultaneously
in the green room but will not be broadcast publicly
until next week. I feel very special
yet out of step with the rest of the viewing world.

In aerobics class we lie on our backs and pump our hips
repetitively towards the ceiling. Soon lovers will come
to smother us with their bodies, pumping equally.
Now there are only our midriffs rising and lowering,
our shapes contained in lycra and cotton.

I break cold medication out of its blister wrap
in the green room, I swallow sedatives in soothing colours.
The makeup person touches my face with gentle fingers.
She covers me in a smock the colour of roses
and together we watch the changes in the mirror.

The faces around me are glazed with perspiration,
their bodies are lovely and plain by turns.
I take my position at the exercise bar between two bodies.
I resume the process of making myself perfect
as they both are, yet not like them, uniquely myself.

I see my body in four funhouse mirrors.
It is shaped exactly like an upended couch.
The gym is a marvel of bodies in motion,
lineups are polite at the popular machines,
active minds are occupied with weight goals, diet instructions.

The audience would wave if the camera glanced their way.
It would stampede to the nearest exit in case of fire
or planted bomb, crushing members of its own sex and race.
I am very calm. I have rehearsed my instructions,
not once do I stray from the script or structure.

Journalists declare there are weather and wars
happening outside the fitness-club doors,
but I hear only music and the splash of water fountains.
I only notice how others have tied back their hair.
Rarely do I look outside, for something other or more.

COACH HOUSE PRESS
50 Prince Arthur Avenue, Suite 107
Toronto, Canada M5R 1B5

Editor for the Press: Lynn Crosbie
Cover Design: Pippa White